Alcohol Addiction
Not Worth the Buzz

ILLICIT AND MISUSED DRUGS

ILLICIT AND MISUSED DRUGS

Alcohol Addiction
Not Worth the Buzz

by Ida Walker

Mason Crest

Mason Crest
370 Reed Road
Broomall, Pennsylvania 19008
www.masoncrest.com

Printed in the Hashemite Kingdom of Jordan.

First printing
9 8 7 6 5 4 3 2 1

Library of Congress Cataloging-in-Publication Data

Walker, Ida.
  Alcohol addiction : not worth the buzz / Ida Walker.
      p. cm. — (Illicit and misused drugs)
Includes bibliographical references and index.
ISBN 978-1-4222-2428-1 (hardcover)
ISBN 978-1-4222-2447-2 (paperback)
ISBN 978-1-4222-2424-3 (series hardcover)
ISBN 978-1-4222-9292-1 (ebook)
1. Alcoholism—History. 2. Alcoholism—Treatment—History.
I. Title.
  HV5025.W255 2012
  616.86'1—dc23
                                        2011032564

Interior design by Benjamin Stewart.
Cover design by Torque Advertising + Design.
Produced by Harding House Publishing Services, Inc.
www.hardinghousepages.com

This book is meant to educate and should not be used as an alternative to appropriate medical care. Its creators have made every effort to ensure that the information presented is accurate—but it is not intended to substitute for the help and services of trained professionals.

CONTENTS

INTRODUCTION

Addicting drugs are among the greatest challenges to health, well-being, and the sense of independence and freedom for which we all strive—and yet these drugs are present in the everyday lives of most people. Almost every home has alcohol or tobacco waiting to be used, and has medicine cabinets stocked with possibly outdated but still potentially deadly drugs. Almost everyone has a friend or loved one with an addiction-related problem. Almost everyone seems to have a solution neatly summarized by word or phrase: medicalization, legalization, criminalization, war-on-drugs.

For better and for worse, drug information seems to be everywhere, but what information sources can you trust? How do you separate misinformation (whether deliberate or born of ignorance and prejudice) from the facts? Are prescription drugs safer than "street" drugs? Is occasional drug use really harmful? Is cigarette smoking more addictive than heroin? Is marijuana safer than alcohol? Are the harms caused by drug use limited to the users? Can some people become addicted following just a few exposures? Is treatment or counseling just for those with serious addiction problems?

These are just a few of the many questions addressed in this series. It is an empowering series because it provides the information and perspectives that can help people come to their own opinions and find answers to the challenges posed by drugs in their own lives. The series also provides further resources for information and assistance, recognizing that no single source has all the answers. It should be of interest and relevance to areas of study spanning biology, chemistry, history, health, social studies and more. Its efforts to provide a real-world context for the information that is clearly presented but not overly simplified should be appreciated by students, teachers, and parents.

The series is especially commendable in that it does not pretend to pose easy answers or imply that all decisions can be made on the basis of simple facts: some challenges have no immediate or simple solutions, and some solutions will need to rely as much upon basic values as basic facts. Despite this, the series should help to at least provide a foundation of knowledge. In the end, it may help as much by pointing out where the solutions are not simple, obvious, or known to work. In fact, at many points, the reader is challenged to think for him- or herself by being asked what his or her opinion is.

A core concept of the series is to recognize that we will never have all the facts, and many of the decisions will never be easy. Hopefully, however, armed with information, perspective, and resources, readers will be better prepared for taking on the challenges posed by addictive drugs in everyday life.

— *Jack E. Henningfield, Ph.D.*

7 What Is Alcohol?

Alcohol has been called a nectar of the gods, a tonic, a holy sacrament, even cough medicine. For many, this form of alcohol—the consumable kind, not the type used to relax muscles or sterilize an area before getting an injection—has played an important role in their passage to adulthood. In some families, alcohol is served regularly as part of family meals. In some families, alcohol has proven to be a destructive force.

There are different types of alcohol, and not all of them are safe for consumption. Alcohol that is safe to drink is called ethanol or ethyl alcohol. When the word "alcohol" is used in this book, this is the type that is meant. Other forms of alcohol include:

- butyl alcohol (butanol). Derived from butane, this type is often used in adhesives and varnishes.
- methyl alcohol (methanol or wood alcohol). This is used in the production of *formaldehyde* and industrial

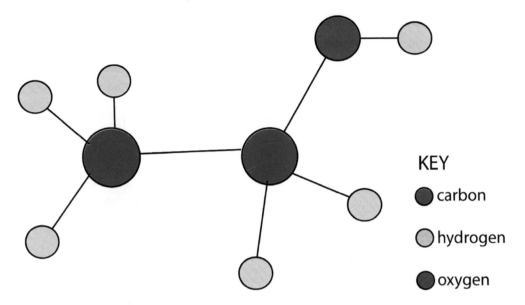

This is the chemical structure of ethyl alcohol. Also called ethanol, it is the only type of alcohol that is safe to drink.

solvents. During **Prohibition**, some people mixed wood alcohol with ethyl alcohol, which led to irreversible blindness in several people because of swelling of the optic nerve.

- isopropyl alcohol. Rubbing alcohol is a common item in many households. It is used as a disinfectant and as an ingredient in colognes and perfumes.
- ethylene glycol. Antifreeze is the most deadly of the alcohols and should never be consumed.

How Is Alcohol Produced?

Alcoholic beverages depend on a chemical change occurring in a substance's molecular structure. In most cases, this happens during a process called fermentation. Fermentation occurs naturally, when yeast present in the air lands on such things as fruit, honey, or grain and feeds off the sugar that is present in them. As the yeast consumes the sugars, carbon dioxide and ethyl alcohol are released. Fermentation stops once the alcohol content reaches a concentration of 14 to 20 percent, because most yeast strains die once the alcohol concentration reaches these levels.

Around the year 800 CE, a process called distillation was developed to boost the potency of alcohol that is intended to be consumed. The mash (consisting of the fruit, grain, or whatever the yeast lands on, as well as that yeast and some water) is boiled. Alcohol boils at a lower temperature than water, so the gas that results from boiling has a higher alcohol content than the mash. This vapor is collected in a special container and cooled back to a liquid form. Once cooled, the liquid that results has a higher alcohol concentration than the original mash.

The level of alcohol in a drink is measured by proof, twice the actual alcohol content of the drink. For

Liquor can be made from many things. Some of them and the resulting product are:

Ingredient	Liquor
rye or potatoes	vodka
molasses or sugarcane	rum
corn	moonshine (corn whiskey)
wheat or rye	whiskey
barley or rice	beer
grapes	wine
apple juice	hard cider
rice	sake

example, 100-proof liquor only contains 50 percent alcohol. (Consuming pure alcohol can quickly cause death; it takes only a few ounces to raise the body's blood alcohol level to the danger zone.) The average alcohol content of some popular liquors are:

- beer: 4.5 percent
- wine: 10–17 percent
- champagne: 12 percent
- distilled spirits: 15 to 50 percent

In the process of distillation, alcohol is evaporated at a lower temperature than water and then recollected in a more concentrated form. Beverages such as whiskey are made in large stills like the ones shown here.

Alcohol is . . .

- a clear liquid when at room temperature.
- less dense than water and boils at a lower temperature (which allows it to be distilled).
- easily dissolved in water.
- flammable, so much so that it can be used as fuel.

There are three main categories of alcoholic beverages: beer, wine, and distilled spirits.

Beer

With its roots in ancient history, beer is one of the oldest, and one of the most popular, alcoholic beverages in the world today. The beer-making process begins with the fermentation of a starch-based substance. Usually this is malted barley, but other areas may use what is native to their region.

Beer's basic ingredients are water, a starch source, and yeast. In most cases, hops are added as flavoring. Beer consists mainly of water, but just ordinary tap water won't do; beer takes on the characteristics of the water being used to make it. Many brew masters believe that hard water, water that contains more minerals, is better suited for dark, heavy flavored beers such as stout. Soft water is used for lighter beers.

Barley malt is the most often used starch source because of its high concentration of amylase, an enzyme that helps the starch break down into sugars. Malt is formed when barley is soaked in water, allowed to begin to *germinate*, and then dried in a kiln. The process creates the enzymes that will eventually turn the starch into sugar that can be fermented.

Hops, a key ingredient in beer brewing, are the dried flowers of the hop plant. They add a bitter flavor and interesting aromas to the beer.

14 Chapter 1—What Is Alcohol?

Hops, dried flowers of the hop plant, became a favorite beer-flavoring agent during the sixteenth century in England. These plants have four characteristics that make them a favorite among beer makers:

1. They lend the bitter flavor that balances the sweetness provided by the malt.
2. They provide distinctive aromas, ranging from flowery to citrus to herbal.
3. They provide an antibiotic effect that allows the brewer's yeast to thrive and helps stop the development of undesirable microorganisms.
4. Hops lengthen the time a beer will hold its "head."

The fermentation process, the step that makes beer beer, depends on the type of yeast selected—ale or lager, which are the two major classifications of beer. The yeast metabolizes the sugars broken down from the starch source, turning the sugars into alcohol and carbon dioxide.

After the beer is brewed, it is bottled and allowed to ripen.

Fast Fact

Contrary to what one might think based on television programs and movies, not all wines improve with age. Sometimes they just get old and some may turn to vinegar.

Wine

The history of wine is almost as long as history itself. It has been consumed for recreational, religious, and even medicinal purposes (more about that in chapter 2). Throughout history, some monasteries have become famous for their vineyards and wine production, even during times when **temperance** or **abstinence** were being encouraged.

Although grapes are most often used for wines, practically any fruit will work. The fruits are crushed (though gone are the days when this was done by people stomping them with their bare feet) and yeast added. The wine is poured into casks or barrels, where it ages. The composition of the barrel will affect the taste of the wine; a **sommelier** might refer to a particular wine's oaken characteristic, for example. How long a wine is allowed to age before bottling depends on many factors, including the type of wine being produced. In general, the darker the wine, the longer the aging process.

Most American wines contain between 10 and 17 percent alcohol. Wines with additional alcohol or brandy added to them are called fortified, and may have an alcohol content of nearly 20 percent.

Fast Fact

One 12-ounce, 10-proof beer is approximately equal to one 5-ounce glass of 24-proof wine, which is equal to a jigger (1.5 ounces) of 80-proof distilled spirits. Each of these drinks has about the same amount of alcohol—0.6 ounces.

Distilled Spirits

The last category of alcoholic beverages is distilled spirits. As mentioned earlier in this chapter, natural fermentation ends when the alcohol content reaches 14 percent. But when Arabs discovered the distilling process, alcoholic beverages with a higher alcohol content—with a harder "kick" to them—could be created. The steam

What About Moonshine?

The American South has a tradition of making and selling illegal corn whiskey—moonshine. Legend has it that the word moonshine (and moonshining) came because the illegal activity was conducted in the night, under the moonlight. Shiners took great precautions in protecting their stills from law enforcement and from competitors.

Though popular images in films and on television often show the moonshiner as being in conflict with the federal tax authorities, racing through the back roads of the rural South trying to outrun the "revenuers," moonshining began long before then. Making moonshine was one way farmers could use up excess corn and grain when their market prices were low.

But there was a lot of racing through the back-country roads during moonshine's heyday, and this practice led to the creation of one of the biggest sports businesses in the world—NASCAR, which also began in the South. One of NASCAR's legendary drivers, Junior Johnson, was almost as famous for outrunning law enforcement while transporting moonshine as he was for his wins on the NASCAR circuit. (He was never caught—driving that is; he was arrested while standing at his father's still.)

Though monetary incentives for making moonshine no longer exist, the practice still continues, especially in some parts of Appalachia. Today's moonshiner, however, is more likely to be attracted by the thrill of the risk-taking than by any financial rewards.

released during distillation, when heating the corn, potato, sugarcane, or whatever substance is used, has more alcohol and less water. Included among distilled liquors are whiskey, rum, brandy, and bourbon.

Wine, beer, and distilled liquor have been a part of everyday life for thousands of years. Though who invented them or when they were first developed might be unclear, what is certain is the impact alcohol has had on the world.

2 The History of Alcohol Use

Though each generation may feel as though it "discovered" alcohol as a rite of passage, drinking alcohol extends back to before recorded history. Besides its use as a beverage for "recreational purposes," alcohol has been an important part of religious ceremonies, a source of vitamins and other nutrients, and has also had medicinal uses. Primitive community members came together to drink alcohol (sound familiar?); alcohol was used to relieve pain and increase appetite. Not everyone shared the same attitude toward the use of alcohol, however. In many civilizations, as use of alcohol spread, so did its abuse, sometimes bringing with it a change in attitudes toward alcohol consumption.

The Beginning of Civilization—The Beginning of Alcoholic Beverages

No one knows for certain when alcohol was first used as a beverage, but *Stone Age* beer jugs discovered on archaeological expeditions show that civilizations fermented beverages during the Neolithic Period (around 10000 BCE). Some researchers believe that beer, rather than bread, may have been civilization's first staple product. Egyptian *pictographs* from around 4000 BCE include images of wine. For citizens of Sumeria, one of the first civilizations, beer and wine were used as medicines as early as 2000 BCE.

Grapes were probably not the first fruits to be used for making alcoholic beverages. Researchers believe that

Dating Systems and Their Meaning

You might be accustomed to seeing dates expressed with the abbreviations BC or AD, as in the year 1000 BC or the year AD 1900. For centuries, this dating system has been the most common in the Western world. However, since BC and AD are based on Christianity (BC stands for Before Christ and AD stands for anno Domini, Latin for "in the year of our Lord"), many people now prefer to use abbreviations that people from all religions can be comfortable using. The abbreviations BCE (meaning Before Common Era) and CE (meaning Common Era) mark time in the same way (for example, 1000 BC is the same year as 1000 BCE, and AD 1900 is the same year as 1900 CE), but BCE and CE do not have the same religious overtones as BC and AD.

The ancient Egyptians drank beer and wine as an important part of everyday life. They also thought it would be as important in the afterlife, as shown by jugs found in burial tombs.

it is more likely that a region's native berries and honey were initially used to make these beverages. The roots of winemaking have been traced to the Middle East.

Ancient Egypt and Babylonia

Ancient Egypt played an important role in the history of alcoholic beverages, and they played an important part in that country's history as well. A *polytheistic* culture, Egypt's local regions and even individual families had their own gods, which they worshipped and honored. Osiris, the god of wine—and many Egyptians felt the inventor of beer as well—was so important that he was worshipped all over Egypt.

In ancient Egypt, beer was treated as a *staff of life*, and each home brewed some almost daily, the first microbreweries. Studies have found that there were at least seventeen varieties of beer and twenty-four kinds of wine. Beer and wine were drunk for pleasure, as well as used as a provider of nutrients, for medicinal purposes, and even as payment for goods and services. Ancient Egyptians also used these beverages as offerings to their gods. One's relationship with alcohol was not believed to end with physical life either; archaeological excavations have found that alcoholic beverages were placed in burial tombs for use in the afterlife.

Moderation was a key concept in the attitude of ancient Egyptians toward drinking alcohol. According to some historians, while widespread moderate use of alcohol was accepted, Egyptians were encouraged not to establish or frequent taverns, since in

Despite alcohol's popularity throughout history, moderation in consumption was practiced as a general rule. Ancient Egyptians were discouraged from frequenting taverns and drunkenness was frowned upon in Babylonia.

addition to serving alcohol, many taverns of the time also served prostitutes. Drunkenness appears not to have been a major problem at the time.

In Babylonia, which was located in the fertile plain between the Euphrates and Tigris rivers, wine and gods were also connected. Wine-associated deities, including a wine goddess, were worshipped as early as 2700 BCE. Both beer and wine were used as offerings in religious rituals, but the beverage of choice for ancient Babylonians was beer.

Moderation in alcohol consumption was practiced by most in Babylonia; *inebriation* was frowned upon, though being drunk was not considered a crime in Babylonia. Although the Code of Hammurabi includes

Alcohol Timeline

6000–4000 BCE	Viticulture is believed to have originated in the mountains between the Black and Caspian seas.
3000–2000 BCE	Beer making flourishes in Sumerian/Mesopotamian civilization with recipes for over twenty varieties of beer recorded on clay tablets.
3000–2000 BCE	Wine production and trade become an important part of Mediterranean commerce and culture.
2200 BCE	Cuneiform tablet recommends beer as a tonic for lactating women.
3000–1000 BCE	Beer is unrefined and usually drunk through a straw because it had large quantities of grain and mash in it.
1800 BCE	Beer is produced in quantity in northern Syria.
1500 BCE	Wine is produced commercially in the Levant and Aegean.
900–800 BCE	Extensive, large-scale vineyards are laid out in Assyria and produce over 10,000 skins of wine for the capital at Nimrud.
800 BCE	Distillation of barley and rice beer is practiced in India.

(Source: Loyola Marymount University. "History of Alcohol Use." http://www.lmu.edu/headsup/students/history.html.)

regulations surrounding "drink," it does not mention drunkenness. Rather, its rules regarding alcohol dealt with its sale—and what would happen if a "sister of a god" (a religious woman) opened or went into a tavern to drink (she would be burned).

China

Alcoholic beverages have been used in all segments of Chinese society since prehistoric times. Although also used for hospitality and as a fatigue fighter, the primary use of alcoholic beverages was in spiritual and religious rituals, as well as in official ceremonies. According to Fei-Peng, quoted on the website www2.potsdam.edu:

> In ancient times people always drank when holding a memorial ceremony, offering sacrifices to gods or their ancestors, pledging resolution before going into battle, celebrating victory, before feuding and official executions, for taking an oath of allegiance, while attending the ceremonies of birth, marriage, reunions, departures, death, and festival banquets.

In ancient China, the main purpose of alcoholic beverages was a part of spiritual and religious ceremonies. In fact, one emperor decreed that heaven condoned the moderate consumption of alcohol.

While most ancient Greeks drank in moderation, followers of Dionysus, the god of wine, drank to the point of intoxication. The Romans also celebrated this god, under the name Bacchus, by overindulging in food and drink.

There was nary a situation in China for which an alcoholic beverage was not considered to be appropriate. As a matter of fact, a ruling by an emperor around 1116 BCE emphasized that even heaven condoned the moderate consumption of alcohol. China's national treasury was also pleased when people drank alcohol; daily consumption of alcohol made it one of the country's biggest income generators.

As in many cultures whose citizens partook of alcohol, China tried to stem its citizens' overindulgence. According to the Drug Addiction Research Foundation of Ontario, between 1100 BCE and 1400 CE, the Chinese government passed and *repealed* forty-one laws prohibiting wine making. However, they eventually saw the *futility* of their efforts. One person writing around 650 BCE said: "[the Chinese] will not do without beer. To prohibit it and secure total abstinence from it is beyond the power even of sages. Hence, therefore, we have warnings on the abuse of it." If the government couldn't stop its citizens from consuming any alcohol, it would do what it could to warn them of the dangers and consequences of drinking too much.

Greece

Mead was the first alcoholic beverage to gain widespread popularity in what is present-day Greece. Winemaking had spread throughout the country by 1700 BCE, and it didn't take long for wine to become a popular beverage of choice. Like other cultures, it was used for rituals and for social occasions, and for medicinal purposes; Hippocrates was among those who believed that wine had medicinal properties. Wine became a regular component of many families' meals. Residents of Greece like their wine warm (or cold), straight (or mixed with water), and plain (or with some native spices added).

Ancient Greeks stressed the importance of drinking in moderation; they even went so far as to recommend temperance. Living a life clouded by a daily fog of alcohol was considered less than moral or desirable. One way many tried to avoid excessive drinking was by watering down the wine. It was not unusual, though, for some ancient Greeks to take advantage—overadvantage—of the wine and other alcoholic beverages readily available at festivals and banquets.

Not all Greeks were agreeable to living a life of moderation or abstinence when it came to drinking. The cult of Dionysus, the god of wine, agriculture, and the fertility of nature (his Roman name is Bacchus), is best known for its willingness to "have a good time." For those who followed Dionysus, drinking to the point of intoxication was their way of getting close to the god. The mother of Alexander the Great, king of the **Macedonians**, was a follower of the cult of Dionysus. The king followed in his mother's footsteps, earning a reputation for his overindulgence of alcohol.

The Hebrews

Captivity in Egypt introduced the Hebrews to wine. When Moses lead them out of Egypt to Canaan circa 1200 BCE, they were pleased with gaining their freedom, but the Bible reports that they were unhappy about leaving behind the plentiful wines (Numbers 20:5). Imagine how happy they must have been to find their new homeland **replete** with vineyards!

But, the Hebrews' stay in Canaan would not be permanent. In 586 BCE, Babylonians conquered the Hebrews,

The Jewish culture values wine as a blessing from God, and therefore something to be enjoyed, but not abused. Wine plays an important role in Jewish culture and rituals, such as the Passover Seder.

and they were deported to Babylon, where they would be forced to stay until Persia captured Babylon and released the Hebrews after almost fifty years of exile. After achieving their newfound freedom, the Hebrews developed Judaism. During the next two centuries, the use of wine as a beverage became widespread, crossing class and age boundaries. Wine was used for its medicinal and nutritional values, as well as consumed for recreation.

Although alcohol had an important place in the Jewish culture, people were encouraged to drink in moderation, not to the point of drunkenness. The Jewish people

Many Romans praised Caesar because he practiced moderation, when most of Roman society was giving in to overindulgence. They saw him as a role model, who would help save Roman society from destruction.

viewed wine as something meant to be treasured as a blessing from God, not something to be abused. Wine became a part of Jewish rituals; around 525 BCE, religious authorities mandated that a blessing over a cup of wine would become part of Kiddish, the prayers signaling the start of **Shabbat** at sundown on Fridays.

Italy

Most historians believe that moderation in all things was widespread in Rome between its founding in 753 BCE and 300 BCE. This all changed when the Romans conquered the peninsula of Italy and the Mediterranean, sometime between 509 and 133 BCE. Although the change in behavior did not occur overnight, the moderation that had characterized life among the Romans gave way to more **decadent** behaviors. **Bacchanals** spread throughout Italy, with practices very similar to their Greek counterparts. Romans began to overindulge in both food and drink; drinking on an empty stomach and self-inducing vomiting to allow consumption of even more drink were not uncommon behaviors. Some historians believe that this period saw the birth of the first drinking games. One game involved consuming as many cups of alcohol as indicated by a throw of the dice.

Eventually, the practice of overindulgence became commonplace throughout Roman society. Its leaders were not immune; Marc Antony even took pride in the bad behaviors caused by his overdrinking. With intoxication becoming the norm, and bad behavior running rampant, some people began to blame the abuse of alcohol for the destruction of the Roman society. These people looked to such leaders as Julius Caesar as their role models. Though not abstinent, Caesar practiced moderation, and many praised him and others like him for their exhibition of self-control.

Early Christianity

The birth of Jesus Christ and subsequent development of Christianity, especially the New Testament of the Bible, greatly influenced attitudes toward alcohol. Some historians note that there are few references to alcohol and drunkenness in the writings shortly after Jesus's death. These historians **hypothesize** that this is because drunkenness was a problem of the upperclass, and Jesus had little contact during his lifetime with such a problem. Others note that Jesus, like many of his era, had no problem with alcohol, even using it in rituals, as long as it was drunk in moderation; he did, however, speak out against drunkenness.

The writings of Saint Paul, who died almost thirty years after Jesus, helped shape Christianity's attitude toward alcohol. As had the Jewish people before him, Paul considered alcohol to be a blessing from God, therefore something to be cherished and used with care. He recommended its use for medicinal purposes, but suggested that anyone who could not control consumption choose to live a life of abstinence. Drunkenness was condemned in both the Old Testament and the New Testament.

Christian **heretics** in the second century disagreed. They called for complete abstinence from drinking alcohol. The Church responded in the fourth and fifth centuries that wine was a gift from God, so it could not be evil; whether someone drank was a personal choice, but to hate wine was to hate one of God's gifts, a sin against Christianity. The Church again spoke out against

Early Christians viewed alcohol as a blessing from God, something to be valued and respected. As demonstrated by the changing of water to wine, Jesus himself had no problems with alcohol, as long as it was used in moderation.

Alcohol Addiction—Not Worth the Buzz

Alcohol use has been important throughout the history of Europe. In Germany local breweries were a source of pride for towns and villages, and in England rent was sometimes paid with beer or ale.

34 Chapter 2—The History of Alcohol Use

drunkenness, however, saying that those who could not practice self-control should live without alcohol.

As Christianity spread throughout Europe, fear spread among some people that their cultures would be consumed by this new belief system. In the early days of Christianity, fearful that they would lose their identity, Jewish leaders established and wrote down practices to keep their cultures alive. Included among these practices was the use of alcohol. Jewish leaders established specific rules about the consumption of alcohol and included them in the Talmud, the collection of ancient Jewish writings that makes up the basis of Jewish religious law. A limited amount of wine would become part of many Jewish ceremonies. Even more rules regarding wine were incorporated into the Talmud during the fifth century. These included rules about how much wine could be drunk on the Sabbath, how the wine was to be drunk, what kinds of wine could be consumed, and personal responsibility for acts committed while intoxicated.

Christianity also influenced Roman culture in the early centuries. After 69 CE, Roman emperors became known for *not* drinking rather than for continuing the alcohol-abusing behaviors of their predecessors. Some historians contend that the raucous, heavy-drinking behaviors of the public became a thing of the past during this period, though some excesses continued for years to come.

The Middle Ages and Beyond

During the Middle Ages and beyond, attitudes toward the use of alcohol continued to evolve. Monasteries and their monks practiced **viticulture**, improving the strains of the grapes; the wine they made from the grapes was used for **mass** and the excess sold to the public. Around 1000, ale and beer were used to pay rent in England. Local breweries became a source of pride to German towns and villages. The process of distillation was also developed during the Middle Ages, opening up a new line of alcoholic beverages. *Aqua vitae*, water of life, was sold as a cure for practically every ailment imaginable; it would later be called brandy.

Although alcohol's use continued and grew, most cultures still stressed the importance of self-control, and if someone couldn't adhere to that, then abstinence was strongly encouraged. In the mid-fourteenth century, however, the Black Death and other plagues in parts of Europe caused many people to become more pessimistic in their approach toward life. Nothing seemed to stop the illnesses and deaths, and many people used alcohol to dull their minds to what was going on. Others felt they had nothing to lose: why not have a good time since they were going to get sick and die anyway. Still others thought that imbibing alcoholic drinks might protect them from this scourge; after all, nothing else seemed to work. And through it all, there were those who believed that moderation in all things would see them through the difficult time.

The Protestant Reformation of the 1500s brought an end to the idea of a single church for the world. Although the basis for Protestant religions might have differed from that of the Catholic Church, the attitudes of the major Protestant leaders of the day toward alcohol were not all that different: alcohol was a gift from God to be used in moderation; drunkenness was sinful. Self-control in all things was emphasized; overindulgence in any aspect of one's life could lead to spiritual crisis and a disruption of society's well-being.

With the widespread use of alcohol in England and Europe, it should be no surprise that it found its way to the New World.

3 Alcohol Comes to the New World

Though early settlers to America's East Coast often have the reputation of being teetotalers who never allowed alcohol to touch their lips, this isn't exactly the true picture. Alcohol came to America when the first European foot stepped on the soil. According to historian H. Lee, Puritan ships sailed to America carrying forty-two tons of beer, fourteen tons of water, and ten thousand gallons of wine! (Some historians claim that the Pilgrims landed where they did because they ran out of beer.) To the Puritans and other early settlers, alcohol was a natural beverage, just like food, but to be consumed in moderation.

The newcomers quickly established alcohol-related businesses. During the 1600s, the colonies' first distillery was built in present-day Staten Island, New York. Hops, integral to making beer, was grown and cultivated in the Massachusetts Colony, and Maryland's early legislature encouraged the development of breweries and distilleries. A very successful rum distillery was established in Boston

> "Drink is in itself a good creature of God, and to be received with thankfulness, but the abuse of drink is from Satan; the wine is from God, but the Drunkard is from the Devil."
> —Puritan minister Increase Mather

in 1657, and it quickly became New England's most prosperous business.

Though the alcohol industry played an important role in the early development of colonies in New England and along the mid-Atlantic, not everyone was pleased with its existence. Some colonies enacted laws limiting who could get alcoholic beverages. For example, in 1637, Massachusetts ordered that no one could stay in a tavern "longer than necessary occasions." And, if you sold alcohol in Plymouth Colony in 1633, you couldn't sell customers more than two-pence worth unless they were newly arrived strangers.

Meanwhile, some people in colonial America wanted to completely outlaw alcoholic beverages, but those efforts were short lived, especially when colonial leaders discovered they could make money from fines. Monetary fines were levied for drunken behavior, selling alcoholic beverages to someone who was already intoxicated or

The Whiskey Rebellion

Government-imposed taxes on popular products and the public's unhappiness about paying them are nothing new. The new government discovered it had a good thing going by charging taxes and fees to the making and selling of alcoholic products. Farmers in western Pennsylvania didn't agree, and attacked revenue collectors in the 1794 Whiskey Rebellion.

Alcohol came over to the New World with the Pilgrims. Though some laws were enacted to help limit alcohol intake, for most people the alcohol industry played an important role in the beginnings of the colonies.

to Native Americans, and for selling alcohol without a proper license or permit. License fees and taxes on liquor added to alcohol-generated revenue.

Attempts to outlaw alcohol beverages resurfaced in the late eighteenth century. One of the first calls for its ban was by minister John Wesley in 1773. A member of the Society of Friends (the Quakers) issued a pamphlet shortly afterward, also calling for its prohibition. John Adams was concerned that taverns were becoming havens for disorderly people. Even arguments touting alcohol's health benefits came under attack. In 1785, Dr. Benjamin Rush wrote that alcohol caused "certain extravagant acts which indicate a temporary fit of madness." Although these early pleas for prohibition were unsuccessful,

The temperance movement originally had limited followers, but it expanded in support until the first prohibition law was enacted in 1843. However, as shown in the image above, not everyone agreed that drinking alcohol was a bad thing.

not everyone was willing to give up on the idea of prohibition.

The Temperance Movement

The early temperance movement was spearheaded by the Methodist Church, whose efforts were joined by the Presbyterian Synod of Pennsylvania and the Society of Friends. They proposed to outlaw the sale and drinking of alcoholic beverages. At first, beer and wine were exempt from the ban. By the mid-1800s, however, these alcoholic beverages were also included in the list of evil drinks.

Not all temperance movements were religion based. In 1778, the Free African Society did not include men who drank alcoholic beverages. Following quickly after were the Organization of Brethren and the Litchfield, Connecticut Association, a group of farmers who wanted to discourage the use of alcohol.

In the early 1800s, temperance took on new life with leaders who included Cotton Mather, John Wesley, and Lyman Beecher. All spoke out strongly against drinking alcohol. The major religious movements of the time— Presbyterian, Methodist, Baptist, and Quakers—continued to strengthen their positions on temperance.

The temperance movement received a significant boost all the way from Ireland when an Irish priest, Father Theobald Matthew, traveled the United States between 1849 and 1851. During his travels, he pledged approximately 600,000 individuals to complete abstinence from drinking alcohol. He was the guest at a White House dinner and a Senate reception, giving nonreligious credence to the temperance movement, something many felt was necessary for the movement to be successful.

Beginning in 1874, with the formation of the Women's Christian Temperance Union (WCTU), women played a large role in the temperance movement. Many women saw alcohol as a threat to the well-being of loved ones and an enemy to be fought.

In 1843, the first Prohibition law was enacted in the territory of Oregon, but was then repealed in 1848. The first state to legislate Prohibition was Maine, in 1847. Delaware was next, but its law was declared unconstitutional. Ohio, Illinois, Rhode Island, Minnesota, Massachusetts, Connecticut, Pennsylvania, and New York all passed Prohibition laws in the next few years. Many never went into effect, being **vetoed** or found to be unconstitutional.

According to many historians, a major reason behind these early Prohibition laws' lack of success was simple: they were not supported by the majority of people living in the United States. The temperance organizations did not have the support they needed to win the minds—and votes—of the populace; many people viewed them as being **extremist**. The leaders of the temperance movement realized they had to change their approach in order to succeed in their goal of ridding the country of alcohol; they had to be able to get their message out farther and faster. To do so, many of the temperance organizations consolidated into larger, more powerful ones.

One of the first major organizations was the American Temperance Society (later the American Temperance Union). Not long after its creation in 1826, it began to establish **auxiliaries** to organize efforts on the local level. By 1835, eight thousand locals were organized and operating in the country.

The Other Side of the Story . . .

Citizens and the liquor industry could be forgiven for being confused about the government's stand on Prohibition at this time. In 1802, federal taxes on liquor began to be repealed; the industry would be tax free between 1818 and 1862. In 1850, the government signed a treaty with the king of Hawaii, which allowed for the importation and sale of liquor there. The medicinal quality of liquor was also being exploited, with medicines such as Lydia Pinkham's Compound containing 40-proof alcohol.

But with the beginning of the Civil War, things began to look not quite so cheerful for the liquor industry. In part to raise money to fight the war, liquor taxes were reinstated and then raised regularly. A strange thing was happening (or not happening), though; the taxes were increased, but the amount of money coming into the federal coffers was not. Fewer and fewer gallons of liquor were being made—or at least being reported as being made. Those in alcohol-related businesses had found loopholes in the tax laws and took full advantage of them. Government attempts to stop, or even limit, the fraud were only marginally successful.

The liquor industry was not just relying on tax evasion as a method of keeping its profits. It looked for other ways to influence government policy on alcohol, and found one by creating a *lobbying* group, the United States Brewers Association. In 1863, this organization was successful in cutting the tax on beer by almost half.

Temperance organizations were a sturdy (some might

Though not as well known today, the Women's Christian Temperance Union still exists. Members are still required to pledge to a life of abstinence from alcohol and other substances. Today's WCTU fights against drug abuse and tobacco use, and continues to educate against alcohol use and abuse.

say stubborn) bunch, and they were not about to give up and let things go on as before. In 1874, both proponents and opponents of Prohibition would meet a mighty force—women.

Women and the Fight for Temperance

Prohibition came along at the right time. In the early 1800s, though women still did not have the right to vote, they were becoming active in issues that affected them, their families, and society as a whole. In the minds of many women, one of the biggest threats to the

Carrie Nation was one of the most famous members of the WCTU. Part of her fight for temperance included destroying saloons with an axe, a practice she termed "hatchetation."

well-being of those around them was liquor, and they were ready to fight—both literally and figuratively. Until the late 1800s, women were on the fringes of involvement in the temperance movement, but with the formation of the Women's Christian Temperance Union (WCTU) in 1874, women's efforts on behalf of temperance took center stage.

The WCTU exemplifies a characteristic of many organizations of the period: it was not limited to one "cause." The organization saw alcohol as a result of bigger social issues, and under the leadership of Frances Willard, it took on other issues of social conscious, including campaigns to get a better Indian policy, prison reform, better sanitary conditions, and civil service reform. It never forgot the original purpose of its founding, however, and concentrated on teaching the public, including children, about alcohol and the dangers of inebriation. The WCTU joined with McGuffey's Readers to educate children about the evils of licensing liquor stores. Every state except Arizona had **compulsory** temperance education in their schools by 1902, largely through the efforts of this partnership.

One of the most recognizable names associated with the WCTU is Carrie Nation. She traveled throughout the United States and into Canada and the British Isles fighting to rid the country of saloons. Almost six feet tall, the sight of her with an ax, ready to demolish singlehandedly any saloon, made many men quake in their shoes.

The Anti-Saloon League

Carrie Nation's activities were not the only ones directed toward saloons. The Anti-Saloon League, founded in 1895, blamed saloons for "annually sending thousands of

As the United States wavered about a Prohibition Law, one of the confusing issues was the fact that alcohol was still thought to have medicinal value. In fact, some patent medicines contained as much as 40 percent alcohol.

Alcohol Addiction—Not Worth the Buzz 49

The Volstead Act was not popular among most citizens, who found ways to get around the law. Part of this crime trend was the increase of organized crime in the United States.

50 Chapter 3—Alcohol Comes to the New World

our youths to destruction, for corrupting politics, dissipating workmen's wages, leading astray 60,000 girls each year into lives of immorality and banishing children from school." League posters called saloon owners "profiteers who feasted on death and enslavement." Unlike organizations such as the WCTU, the League did not delve into other social ills, keeping its eyes and efforts sharply focused on the elimination of alcohol.

The Volstead Act

As the nineteenth century turned into the twentieth, the movement toward Prohibition remained strong. Women were powerful proponents. Factory owners also wanted Prohibition; they needed workers willing—and able—to work long hours. Many religious organizations backed Prohibition as a way to rid the world of an evil. Scientists were casting doubts on the medicinal qualities of alcohol, and in 1915, whiskey and brandy were removed from the United States **Pharmacopoeia**.

Temperance organizations had been successful in getting their message to the states. Between 1905 and 1917, states passed laws prohibiting the manufacture and sale of alcoholic beverages. Finally, in 1917, members of the U.S. Congress hopped on the bandwagon and passed the Eighteenth Amendment, Prohibition, which outlawed the manufacture, sale, or transportation of intoxicating liquors in the United States. The amendment was sent to the state legislatures for **ratification**; approval by three-fourths of the states was required for the amendment to become law. Although seven years was allowed to accomplish ratification, it was complete in only thirteen months; Mississippi was the first state to ratify the amendment, and Nebraska put the total over the top.

On October 28, 1919, Congress enacted the National Prohibition Act—the Volstead Act—which put the amendment into effect, and on January 17, 1920, the country went "dry." (Wine was still allowed in the practice of Jewish and Catholic religious rites.)

At first, everything seemed to go as Prohibition supporters had claimed it would. The consumption of liquor dropped dramatically. The number of alcohol-related arrests fell. Reflecting the economic principle of supply and demand, the price of illegal alcohol skyrocketed, keeping it out of reach of the average citizen.

That's what happened at first. But then people became quite inventive at going around the law. Bootlegging became rampant; people carried liquor in hollowed-out canes, books, and hip flasks; the number of *speakeasies* in the big cities grew and grew. Organized crime became involved in manufacturing, transporting, and selling illegal liquor, and violence increased. Whiskey was still available by prescription, and in 1928, doctors earned an estimated $40 million by writing prescriptions for the spirit. Liquor was smuggled across the Canadian border without difficulty. New forms of alcoholic beverages were being made, such as near-beer and fermented fruit juices. Grape-growers produced Vine-go; by adding water, one could have a strong wine in just two months.

There were laws, federal, state, and local, but in most cases, they were not enforced equally across the country. Though Prohibition proved effective in the South and West, it was pretty much a lost cause in the nation's big cities and in small towns where miners and industrial workers lived.

Efforts to repeal Prohibition began almost immediately after its passage. To counter the efforts of the WCTU, the

Women's Organization for National Prohibition Reform was organized. They declared that Prohibition was wrong in principle. The Association Against the Prohibition Amendment (AAPA) financed many of the repeal efforts, and did so effectively. AAPA looked toward changing the makeup of Congress to better their chances of repealing the Eighteenth Amendment and worked hard to elect representatives and senators who supported the repeal. Ending Prohibition became an issue in the 1928 presidential election. Alfred E. Smith supported repeal, but the eventual winner, Herbert Hoover, called it a "great social and economic experiment," and Prohibition stayed in place with his election win.

But when Hoover left the White House, Prohibition's end could be seen on the horizon. The amendment to repeal Prohibition was introduced on February 14, 1933. The Senate and the House passed the amendment in just six days. Michigan was the first state to ratify the amendment, and ratification was complete on November 7, 1933, with the approval of Kentucky, Ohio, Pennsylvania, and Utah. Congress officially adopted the Twenty-First Amendment on December 5, 1933. Prohibition was over.

People who favored Prohibition, including those in the U.S. government who passed the amendment, believed they were doing what was best for individuals. They did not believe people had the self-control needed to handle the "evilness" of drink. In order to make informed decisions, to exhibit self-control, it is necessary to know how alcohol can have such a strong power over an individual.

4 How Alcohol Affects the Body

I had always been painfully shy. In the past I'd felt ignored and left out by this group of older kids. But, as soon as I drank the beer, everything seemed wonderful. I was no longer shy; I could talk to people, dance and sing. Everybody seemed to like me and find me fun to be with.

The above story is told by Cathy C. on the website www.legacyaa.com. Her story is not unique, as many people perceive alcohol to be beneficial because it makes them more at ease in social situations. Unfortunately, for many, their use doesn't stop there, and drinking becomes a problem for them and those around them. But there is no doubt that alcohol does change behavior, and to understand how it can become a problem, it is necessary to first understand how alcohol works on the body.

Alcohol and the Body

When someone has an alcoholic drink, the stomach absorbs about 20 percent of the alcohol; the remaining 80 percent is absorbed by the small intestine. How quickly the body absorbs alcohol depends on:

- the amount of alcohol in the drink
- the type of drink (carbonated beverages such as soda speed up the absorption of alcohol)
- the amount of food in the stomach (food slows down absorption)

You can find out estimated BAC levels on the website www.ou.edu/oupd/bac.htm. Here are a couple of calculations:

1. Number of drinks	3
2. What are you drinking?	5 oz. wine
3. How much do you weigh?	140 lbs.
4. How many hours have you been drinking?	2 hrs.
BAC	0.03

Another example:

1. Number of drinks	6
2. What are you drinking?	12 oz. beer
3. How much do you weigh?	140 lbs.
4. How many hours have you been drinking?	3 hrs.
BAC	0.08

Both of these BAC levels indicate possible impairment.

How alcohol affects the body depends on a number of factors. For example, alcohol that is consumed with food will be absorbed more slowly than alcohol that hits an empty stomach.

- how accustomed one is to drinking
- the individual's size, weight, and gender (women are generally affected more quickly because they are smaller than men)

After being absorbed, the alcohol enters the bloodstream and dissolves in the blood's water. The alcohol travels through the body, entering and dissolving in each tissue (except fat) of the body. Once the alcohol has entered the tissues, its effects begin to be experienced. What effects an individual feels depends on the blood alcohol concentration (BAC), a calculation based on number of drinks, what was drunk, weight, and hours spent drinking. Most effects will begin to be experienced between ten and twenty minutes after taking the drink.

Once the alcohol has entered the bloodstream, the kidneys and lungs eliminate a small percentage; the liver breaks down 90 percent in a process called oxidation. An enzyme called alcohol dehydrogenase removes the *electrons* from the alcohol, creating acetaldehyde. The breakdown is complete when another enzyme, aldehyde dehydrogenase, uses oxygen to convert acetaldehyde to acetic acid (the main ingredient in vinegar).

Alcohol and the Brain

Alcohol passes directly from the digestive tract into the brain, crossing the *blood–brain barrier*. Alcohol is a depressant, which means its effects slow down mental and

Women, because they are usually lighter and smaller than men, will feel the effects of alcohol more quickly than men. Because of this, it can be dangerous for women to try and "keep up" with men when drinking alcohol.

physical functioning. When alcohol reaches the brain, it affects the brain's complex communication system by acting on its nerve cells, or neurons. These neurons are the messengers responsible for passing along the information from cell to cell. Each nerve cell consists of a cell body with an axon, a whip-like tail at one end, and root-looking projections called dendrites at the other end. Because neurons do not touch each other, impulses from one neuron hop aboard neurotransmitters found in the synapses, the spaces between nerve endings, to get a ride to the receptors on the next neuron.

Neurotransmitters either **excite** or **inhibit** receiving neurons. In the case of alcohol, the neurotransmitter involved is gamma-aminobutyric acid (GABA), an inhibitor. Alcohol increases the effects of GABA, causing actions to become sluggish. Alcohol also weakens the neurotransmitter glutamine, which is an excitatory neurotransmitter. Inhibiting the actions of this neurotransmitter also creates sluggishness.

As a person's BAC increases, the effect on the brain increases. The cerebral cortex—the part of the brain responsible for processing sensory information, thought processing, consciousness, and initiating voluntary muscle movements—feels the effects of alcohol first. Alcohol depresses the behavioral inhibitory centers, causing the person to become more talkative, less shy (like Cathy at the beginning of the chapter); slows down the processing of sensory information, which causes problems seeing, touching, and tasting; and inhibits thought processes, impairing judgment. The higher the BAC, the more the cerebral cortex is affected.

The limbic system is the next part of the brain to feel alcohol's impact. This is the area of the brain that

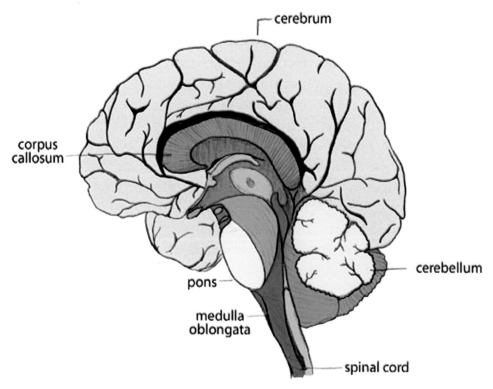

cerebrum

corpus
callosum

cerebellum

pons

medulla
oblongata

spinal cord

In the brain, alcohol first affects the cerebral cortex, the part of the brain that is responsible for processing sensory information, thought processing, and initiating voluntary muscle movements. The diminished senses and impaired judgment will continue to get worse as more alcohol is consumed.

controls emotions and memories. Someone under the influence may feel exaggerated emotional states—rage or extreme sadness, for example—and a loss of memory.

When the cerebellum is affected, someone under the influence of alcohol begins to lose motor skills. The cerebellum controls fine movements; tasks that would normally be completed with no difficulty—such as touching a finger to the nose with eyes closed, one of the field sobriety tests used by law enforcement—become more difficult. Movements become jerky, and with higher levels of BAC, the person becomes uncoordinated and may find walking difficult, if not impossible.

Alcohol also affects the hypothalamus, the area of the brain that coordinates the output of **endocrine** glands. BAC depresses areas in the hypothalamus that control sexual arousal and performance. Sexual inhibition decreases as the BAC level rises. However, the ability to perform sexually also decreases as BAC increases, creating somewhat of a dilemma.

Involuntary functions such as breathing, heart rate, consciousness, and temperature are controlled by the medulla (brain stem). When the effects of alcohol reach the upper levels of the medulla, the person will begin to feel sleepy, and if the BAC is high enough, he may eventually pass out. When a person has consumed a large amount of alcohol and has a high BAC, the respiration rate can become very slow (the person can actually stop breathing), and the heart rate can also slow drastically, causing blood pressure and body temperature to drop to dangerously low, potentially fatal levels.

Alcohol and the Rest of the Body

Alcohol's effects are not limited to the brain. Some effects are more serious than others, but all should be considered when weighing the option of whether to drink:

Appearance

According to experts, having more than a couple of drinks a week promotes aging of the skin. Replacing nutritional calories with the non-nutritional ones found in alcohol can cause hair to become brittle, lips to crack, and give skin a puffy, broken vein appearance. Alcohol can also increase the severity and frequency of acne breakouts. It increases blood flow to the skin as well, making someone sweat and look flushed.

Gastrointestinal Tract

Heartburn and stomach ulcers can result from alcohol intake. Links have been made between alcohol use and cancers of the mouth, esophagus, stomach, and intestines. Of course the liver suffers the most damage, since it is the workhorse in the alcohol elimination process. Cirrhosis, a liver disease often found in people who abuse alcohol, can be fatal.

Muscles

Alcohol causes the reduction of blood flow to the muscles. This can cause severe muscle cramps.

FAST FACT
Only time will make alcohol's effects wear off—and it can't be rushed. A cold shower won't help, and neither will multiple cups of coffee; all you'll end up with is a wet, wide-awake person feeling the effects of alcohol.

If a lot of alcohol has been consumed, when the effects reach the brain stem, the individual will become sleepy and may pass out. In some cases, breathing and heart rate can slow to dangerously low levels, sometimes even stopping completely.

Despite alcohol's potential negative effects, many people drink and experience no problems. However, there are people for whom drinking alcoholic beverages becomes more than a question of an occasional hangover. For them, alcohol is a necessity in their lives, something they can't live without.

5 Alcohol Addiction: Alcoholism

My mom and dad always let us kids take sips of their drinks, ever since we were about twelve or thirteen. It wasn't a big deal. Then when I got older, my friends starting drinking beer at parties, and I joined in. It was just this thing I did to be cool, to fit in. Ended up, by my senior year, I was getting drunk most weekends, not because I really liked the way it made me feel, but just because there were a lot of parties going on and I was having a good time with my friends.

Then I went to college. There were still plenty of parties going on, and I still wanted to have fun—but I wanted to get good grades more. I really couldn't do both, not with a pre-med major. So I eased up on the drinking, and finally quit altogether. Now, I'll have a glass of wine if someone takes me out to dinner, or a beer with a pizza on a Saturday afternoon when I have a chance to kick back. I don't really drink. I mean I don't get drunk. I haven't for years now. It was just a waste of time, from my perspective. (Terri, age twenty-two, Internet chatroom)

I had my first drink when I was 15. Everyone else was doing it, so why not. I couldn't stop though. At first I just drank on weekends hanging out with the guys. Before I knew it, though, I was grabbing a drink between classes from a little bottle I kept in my sneaker in my locker. Then some of us started cutting out on lunch and grabbing a beer [a friend's brother] bought. Well, it got harder and harder to go to class in the afternoon. I did graduate, though, but just by the skin of my teeth. (Mark, age twenty, Internet chatroom)

Terri's and Mark's stories show two sides of the alcohol coin. There are some people who can drink occasionally and not have a problem. Others, however, can't control their alcohol intake, and it becomes a serious problem affecting all areas of their lives.

Many adults have a drink or two a day, often as part of dinner. However, there are some people who cannot stop at just two drinks and are at risk for alcohol abuse.

The overwhelming majority of people who drink alcohol do so socially, as a part of dinner, for example. For most adults, up to two drinks a day for men and one drink a day for women and senior citizens is not harmful; it is considered moderate alcohol use. For the others, an estimated 17.6 million adult Americans, that same amount is too much: once they start with those one or two drinks a day, they can't stop. They have a problem with alcohol abuse, and potentially, alcohol addiction.

Someone who abuses alcohol does not have the craving, loss of control or physical dependence on alcohol seen in someone with addiction. However, he may still drink too much at inappropriate times, and have legal problems as a result.

Definitions

Although each is serious, not all alcohol-related problems are the same. The most serious is alcohol dependence or alcohol addiction—alcoholism, in other words, no matter what other name you want to give it.

The National Institute on Alcohol Abuse and Alcoholism (NIAA) lists the following symptoms of alcohol addiction:

- craving: a strong need, or compulsion, to drink
- loss of control: the inability to limit one's drinking on any given occasion

- physical dependence: withdrawal symptoms, such as nausea, sweating, shakiness, and anxiety, occur when alcohol use is stopped after a period of heavy drinking
- tolerance: the need to drink greater amounts of alcohol in order to "get high"

For a person with alcoholism, the craving for a drink becomes the overwhelming motivation for getting through the day. It's not a matter of saying yes or no to a drink; the need is so strong that the question is never even asked.

Other people (including many teens) exhibit characteristics of misusing alcohol but do not have the strong craving, loss of control, or physical dependence seen in those with an alcohol addiction. The NIAA define alcohol abuse as a pattern of alcohol consumption that results in one or more of the following within one twelve-month period:

- failure to fulfill major work, school, or home responsibilities;
- drinking in situations that are physically dangerous, such as while driving a car or operating machinery;
- having recurring alcohol-related legal problems, such as being arrested for driving under the influence of alcohol or for physically hurting someone while drunk; and
- continued drinking despite having ongoing relationship problems that are caused or worsened by the drinking.

Alcoholics may also face many of these same issues.

The Causes of Alcoholism

It's a simple fact: anyone who drinks can develop alcoholism or alcohol abuse. Simply drinking steadily over time can create dependence and cause withdrawal symptoms if alcohol is removed. Other factors generally are instrumental in the development of alcoholism: genetics, biology, and culture.

Genetics

Many studies have shown a *genetic* link to alcoholism. Some researchers contend that up to half of someone's risk factors for developing alcoholism can be attributed to genetics. Unlike other conditions with a genetic cause, scientists doubt that a single gene will be identified as the "malfunctioning" one responsible for alcoholism; the disease is simply too complex. Genetic studies of alcoholism have found:

- the amygdala, the area of the brain believed to play a role in the emotional aspects of craving, is smaller in those with a family history of alcoholism.
- a genetic deficiency of acetaldehyde, found in Asians and Jewish populations, may allow a buildup of acetate after drinking alcohol, which can cause flushing, dizziness, and nausea after drinking. These unpleasant experiences may discourage people from developing a dependency on alcohol.
- some people who have alcoholism may also have abnormal levels of serotonin, a neurotransmitter. Abnormal serotonin levels are associated with high tolerance levels for alcohol and can affect impulsive behaviors, which can make individuals more likely to drink, and drink a great deal.

Even with the knowledge that some people can have a genetic predisposition to alcoholism, it is impossible to determine who will actually develop the disorder.

Biology

Researchers are studying how long-term alcohol use changes brain chemistry to allow it to deal with cravings and withdrawal symptoms. Studies have indicated that long-term alcohol use eventually seems to deplete

Everyone who takes a drink is at risk for developing an addiction to alcohol. However, some researchers contend that up to half of the risk factors for becoming an alcoholic are the result of genetics.

the brain's supply of the neurotransmitters dopamine and serotonin, so continued drinking has no physical effect on mood. The individual only *believes* that drinking more will improve mood.

Culture

The glamorous actor or singer appears in a glossy magazine holding a drink, talking about how wonderful life is. Songs relate the wonderful things that happen after

Alcohol advertisements are specifically targeted toward a young audience. They try to encourage the drinking of their product by implying that it will make you happy, cooler, and more fun.

College Culture Drinking Myths

I can drink and still be in control.
Fact: Drinking impairs your judgment, which increases the likelihood that you'll do something that you'll later regret such as having unprotected sex, being involved in date rape, damaging property, or being victimized by others.

Drinking isn't all that dangerous.
Fact: One in three 18- to 24-year-olds admitted to emergency rooms for serious injuries is intoxicated. And alcohol is also associated with homicides, suicides, and drownings.

I can sober up quickly if I have to.
Fact: It takes about 3 hours to eliminate the alcohol content of two drinks, depending on your weight. Nothing can speed up this process—not even coffee or cold showers.

It's okay for me to drink to keep up with my boyfriend.
Fact: Women process alcohol differently. No matter how much he drinks, if you drink the same amount as your boyfriend, you will be more intoxicated and more impaired.

I can manage to drive well enough after a few drinks.
Fact: About one-half of all fatal crashes among 18- to 24-year-olds involve alcohol. If you are under 21, driving after drinking any alcohol is illegal and you could lose your license. The risk of a fatal crash for drivers with positive BACs compared with other drivers increases more steeply for drivers younger than age 21 than for older drivers.

I'd be better off if I could learn to "hold my liquor."
Fact: If you have to drink increasingly larger amounts of alcohol to get a "buzz" or to get "high," you are developing tolerance. Tolerance is actually a warning sign that you're developing more serious problems with alcohol.

Beer doesn't have as much alcohol as hard liquor.
A 12-ounce bottle of beer has the same amount of alcohol as a standard shot of 80-proof liquor (either straight or in a mixed drink) or 5 ounces of wine.

(*Source:* National Institute on Alcohol Abuse and Alcoholism)

a drink. Media stories repeatedly extol the benefits of moderate drinking. Commercials for sweet, malt-based, carbonated, "alcopops" with names like Breezer, are targeted toward a young audience. And college life is often built around a culture that equates good times with alcohol consumption. Clearly, culture plays a major role in encouraging people to drink.

Although these research areas may help determine what causes alcoholism, it doesn't mean that someone under the influence of all of those factors, including a genetic predisposition, will automatically develop alcoholism.

Who Develops Alcoholism?

According to the website Reuters Health (www.reutershealth.com/wellconnected/doc56.html), up to half of American men have problems that can be traced to alcohol, and between 10 percent and 20 percent of men and 3 percent to 10 percent of women either become alcohol abusers or alcoholics. Although each person is different, with different contributing factors, over the years, research has been able to reach some conclusions about who is most likely to develop alcoholism.

Fast Fact
In 2010, 67 percent of all Americans over age eighteen were current drinkers of alcohol. Beer was the preferred drink.

(Source: July 2010 Gallup Poll)

Age

Studies have shown that the longer someone drinks, the more likely the person is to develop alcoholism. It follows, then, that if an individual begins drinking while a teenager (or even younger), he or she will be at an increased risk of developing alcoholism. Adolescents at highest risk for developing alcoholism have other risk factors as well,

Some people begin having problems with alcohol as they get older. This is because as the person ages and his metabolism slows, his body cannot process alcohol in the same way as when he was younger.

According to the National Institute on Alcohol Abuse and Alcoholism, if you are concerned that your family history may increase your possibility of developing alcoholism, you can take the following steps to reduce the chance:

• Avoid underage drinking. Alcoholism rates are higher for people who started drinking at a young age.
• Drink moderately as an adult. Keep in mind that for someone with a family history of alcoholism, even this might be too much. It can be hard to keep drinking at that level.
• Talk to a health-care professional. If your health-care professional is aware of your concerns, he can recommend groups that can help you deal with alcohol.

including a history of abuse, family violence, and depression. Youth with a family history of alcoholism also tend to begin drinking at a young age and eventually become alcoholic.

Simply having wine at dinner does not necessarily mean that the young person will become an alcoholic. Children from families with a cultural tradition of serving wine at family meals do not have a higher incidence of alcoholism.

For some people, alcoholism doesn't develop until their senior years. **Metabolism** changes as a normal part of the aging process. Most people know that eating habits often have to change because an older body doesn't process foods in the same way, and individuals often aren't as active as they age; a woman who maintained a lean and healthy body on 2,000 calories at age thirty might have to reduce her caloric intake at age sixty or find herself with high blood pressure and a few extra pounds. The same is true with alcohol. Individuals who have the same drinking patterns throughout life could find themselves developing alcoholism as they age.

Gender

Although most alcoholics are men, the rate of alcoholism in women is increasing. Historically, women have followed the drinking patterns of their partners, but some evidence indicates that this is changing somewhat as more women delay relationships to pursue careers. Alcoholism tends to develop later in women.

Family History

According to Reuters Health, sons of alcoholic fathers are 25 percent more likely to develop alcoholism at some

Many people enjoy a cup of coffee every morning. However, research has shown that craving substances like caffeine or sugar can indicate a risk of developing alcoholism.

Though more men are alcoholics, the rate of alcoholism in women is increasing. Women tend to develop their problems with alcohol later in life than men.

78 Chapter 5—Alcohol Addiction: Alcoholism

point in their lives. The familial link was less solid for women, but those who did develop alcoholism tended to come from families with parents who drank.

Ethnicity

African Americans, Caucasians, and Hispanics all appear to have similar rates of alcoholism. However, an increased likelihood of developing alcoholism occurs in those of Irish and Native American heritage. Alcoholism rates in Asian and Jewish populations are low, perhaps due to the way alcohol is metabolized.

Cravings for Other Substances

Some studies have shown that people who crave other substances, such as sugar, tobacco, and caffeine, may have a higher risk for developing alcoholism. What is not clear is whether long-term drinking causes an individual to crave those substances, or if craving caffeine, sugar, or tobacco can be used as an indicator for developing alcoholism.

Symptoms and Diagnosis of Alcoholism

According to the Cleveland Clinic, symptoms of alcoholism in its early stages may include:

- drinking for relief from problems
- need for more and more alcohol to feel drunk
- "blackouts": not being able to remember events or blocks of time that happened while drinking
- hiding alcohol or sneaking drinks
- thinking more and more about alcohol
- planning activities around drinking

If you are concerned that you may be at risk for developing alcoholism, watch for early warning signs. One of these early symptoms is thinking about alcohol all the time, so that it interferes with your regular daily activities.

As alcoholism progress to the middle to late stages, these symptoms occur:

- drinking more than planned
- not admitting to having a drinking problem
- trying to control drinking by using mind games, such as deciding never to drink before noon
- breaking promises
- having personality changes and mood swings
- drinking as soon as they wake from a night's sleep

At alcoholism's latest stages, this symptom is common:

- having severe withdrawal symptoms such as delirium tremors (DTs)

People with alcoholism may exhibit all or some of those symptoms. But the number-one symptom of alcoholism—an overpowering need for alcohol—is the one that all alcoholics experience. Even when the individual sees what it is doing to him and to those around him, filling the craving for alcohol is still his primary goal.

The diagnostic process for alcoholism usually begins when the individual hasn't been able to have a drink for a while, and withdrawal symptoms appear. They may include:

- fever
- rapid heartbeat
- increase or decrease in blood pressure
- extremely aggressive behavior
- hallucinations and other mental disturbances
- seizures
- DTs (which develop two to four days after the last drink)

Even with those symptoms staring her in the face, the individual will often deny she has a problem. Of course, by then, the problem has generally become glaring to her family and others close to her. Those who care about the individual must then recognize the symptoms of alcohol withdrawal and encourage her to seek treatment.

Physicians who suspect that a patient might have alcoholism will ask a series of questions to confirm or reject the diagnosis. Besides asking about past and present drinking habits, the physician can use a series of brief tests to aid in diagnosis. Because people with alcoholism are prone to denying their condition, the tests were designed to get answers about problems related to drinking, not about drinking habits.

CAGE Test

The CAGE test is the quickest. Its acronym stands for these words:

- Attempts to CUT (C) down on drinking
- ANNOYANCE (A) with criticisms about drinking
- GUILT (G) about drinking
- Use of alcohol as an EYE-OPENER (E) in the morning

This test appears most accurate in diagnosing alcoholism in white, middle-aged men.

T-ACE Test

This four-question test has a high accuracy rate in detecting alcoholism in men and women.

- Does it TAKE (T) more than three drinks to make you feel high?
- Have you ever been ANNOYED (A) by people's criticism of your drinking?

A doctor who suspects that her patient has a drinking problem will ask questions and use simple tests to come to a diagnosis. Because most alcoholics will deny their problem, she cannot ask them directly.

Alcohol Addiction—Not Worth the Buzz 83

A diagnosis of alcoholism may also reached if the patient has physical symptoms after a long break from drinking. A fever, rapid heartbeat and hallucinations are some examples of these symptoms of withdrawal.

84   Chapter 5—Alcohol Addiction: Alcoholism

- Are you trying to CUT DOWN (C) on drinking?
- Have you ever used alcohol as an EYE-OPENER (E) in the morning?

A "yes" to any two of those four questions indicates possible alcoholism.

A physician won't make a definitive diagnosis based on merely the answers to those screening tests. She'll also perform physical tests to rule out any other medical conditions with symptoms that might mimic alcoholism. Tests for alcohol-related conditions will also be conducted. Should the screenings and tests tell the physician that her patient has a problem related with alcohol, she and the patient's family will work toward getting the patient into treatment. Untreated alcoholism is a dangerous, potentially fatal disease.

The Dangers of Alcoholism

Each year, approximately 25,000 deaths can be attributed to alcohol, excluding thousands more accidents and homicides that are alcohol-related. Someone with alcoholism can expect to have his life cut short by ten to fifteen years. The dangers go beyond the alcoholic, however, and affect those around him.

Effects on the Body

Because alcohol enters the bloodstream so quickly and affects so many areas, scientists have had difficulty determining them all. According to Reuter's Health, some of the most definite ones are:

- Alcoholism can kill in many different ways, and, in general, people who drink regularly have a higher rate

A woman who drinks heavily while pregnant is not only harming her own body. Her baby is drinking as well, and may be born with Fetal Alcohol Syndrome, which can lead to facial deformities and lifetime learning disabilities.

of death from injury, violence, and some cancers.

- Frequent, heavy drinking is associated with a higher risk for alcohol-related medical disorders (*pancreatitis*, upper gastrointestinal bleeding, nerve damage, and *impotence*) than is *episodic* drinking or continuous drinking without intoxication.
- As people age, it takes fewer drinks to become intoxicated, and organs can be damaged by smaller amounts of alcohol than in younger people. Also, up to one-half of the hundred most prescribed drugs for older people react adversely with alcohol.
- Alcohol abusers who require surgery also have an increased risk of *postoperative* complications, including infections, bleeding, insufficient heart and lung functions, and problems with wound healing. Alcohol withdrawal symptoms after surgery may impose further stress on the patient and hinder recuperation.

And those are the ones they know about!

Accidents

Alcohol is a factor in more than one-half of all motor vehicle accidents. A BAC of more than .08 makes one legally impaired, but for some people, a lower level could be just as deadly. Alcohol also makes one vulnerable to injuries from falls and fights.

Suicide, Murder, and Domestic Violence

According to the American Foundation for Suicide Prevention, alcohol is a factor in about 30 percent of suicides. This does not necessarily mean that the individual was intoxicated at the time of suicide. Rather, the person could have been in such despair over her condition

Alcohol is involved in at least a third of all motor vehicle accidents. Not only is it illegal to drive with a BAC over .08, but it can also be fatal.

that suicide seemed the only answer to her problems. The same study showed that alcohol was a factor in almost 70 percent of all murders.

Domestic violence is a major problem in society, and alcohol exacerbates the situation. Research has indicated that a domestic partner with a history of alcohol abuse is the most serious risk factor for physical abuse. Children are also at risk of physical injury from an alcohol-abusing parent, and they are also at increased risk of repeating the abusive behavior when they become adults. These children have less success at school, are more depressed, have fewer friends, and lower self-esteem than their peers. Those characteristics do not bode well for a fulfilling and happy life as an adult.

Fetal Alcohol Syndrome

Women who continue to drink while pregnant run the very real risk of giving birth to a baby with Fetal Alcohol Syndrome (FAS) or any of the other conditions that can result from a mother continuing to drink during pregnancy. According to the National Organization on Fetal Alcohol Syndrome, babies born with this condition may have some, or most, of the following characteristics:

- facial deformities
- *neurodevelopment* disorder
- an abnormally small head circumference (below the 10th percentile)
- intellectual impairment
- memory problems
- delayed development
- *attachment* concerns
- *attention deficit disorder*
- impaired motor skills
- hyperactivity
- *neurosensory* hearing loss
- problems with reasoning and judgment
- learning disabilities
- inability to appreciate consequences
- impaired visual/spatial skills

These are conditions that last a lifetime.

6 Teens and Alcohol

Lots of teenagers start drinking because they like the way it makes them feel. Because it's such a common adolescent activity, it almost seems "normal." But the consequences can be serious.

According to the National Survey on Drug Use and Health (NSDUH), in 2009, an estimated 10.4 million persons aged twelve to twenty reported drinking alcohol in the past month; 2.1 million reported themselves as heavy drinkers. That's a lot of kids drinking (illegally, by the way). The same survey found that 12 percent of people over age twelve reported that they had driven under the influence of alcohol at least once in the past year (also illegal).

Of course kids have been drinking alcohol while underage for many, many years. But today, science and medicine have a far greater understanding of the consequences of adolescent alcohol use. Researchers haven't been keeping their findings a secret—and yet with all the information about why it's a bad idea, kids still do it. Before behavior can be changed, it must be understood.

Why Kids Drink

"Everybody Else Does!"

> When I started high school, I felt so out of place. I was an outsider, coming from the south side, invading the prestigious high school on the wealthy north side of the city.
>
> I did manage to get invited to a party early in the school year. There were a few people I knew, and they were drinking. Actually, it seemed as though everyone had a beer. They seemed to fit in, so I decided to have a beer, too. It's not like it was the first time. My parents gave me sips when they drank. Well, having a beer got to be a regular thing at these parties. You walked in the room and someone hands you a beer. (Sari, age nineteen, Internet chatroom)

One of the most common reasons teenagers offer as an explanation for any particular behavior is "Well, everyone else is doing it." (Does anyone's parents still respond to that with "And if so-and-so jumped off a bridge. . ."?)

When it comes to alcohol, though, it's easy to see how teens reach that conclusion. TV, the Internet, magazines, movies, all seem to connect alcohol and drinking with having a good time, fitting in, having fun.

Escape and Self-Medication

The teenage years are a time of change. One minute things are wonderful, followed shortly by a period of tremendous *angst*. Hormones are running through male and female bodies driving them—and their parents—crazy. It is a time of extreme highs.

In the 2009 NSDUH, 2.1 million teens reported themselves as heavy drinkers. This is defined as having five or more drinks on the same occasion on each of five or more days in the past thirty days.

But it can also be a period of extreme disappointments. "You don't understand," is an all-too-common mantra for adolescents, and whether it's true or not, the feeling is very real. Just as adults often do when they feel lonely and depressed, teenagers may resort to self-medicating; for many, the "medication" of choice is alcohol. When a teen feels she has no one who will understand her problems, she might turn to alcohol to feel better. And she probably will feel better, at least for a while. But when the alcohol's effects wear off, the problems return, sometimes worse than they were before. Without intervention, a vicious circle can begin with problems being dulled by alcohol, returning, and increasing amounts of alcohol consumed in order to forget about the problems, if ever so briefly.

Adolescence is a time of many changes. As her body changes and hormones rage, a teen may feel alone and depressed.

Rebellion

Most teens go through a rebellious period. For some, it might be limited to not cleaning their bedrooms. Others might commit acts of violence. Many teens turn to alcohol when they feel angry and have no way to express their feelings; as the alcohol diminishes their inhibitions, it allows them to act out the aggression they might otherwise control. Others who use alcohol as their rebellion of choice do so simply because Mom and Dad told them not to.

Availability

The media often contains stories about convenience store clerks caught selling alcohol to underage customers. Tales about how to get false IDs and whose brother or sister is willing to buy alcohol for their underage siblings and their friends are common in high schools. Indeed, that is how some underage teens get their alcohol. But for most teens, it's not that complicated. They get it from their parents' liquor cabinet, or their parents buy it for them.

Most people in America drink, so it makes sense that many homes would have alcohol in them. Most teens know how to steal a drink of whiskey or some clear alcoholic beverage without their parents noticing. Or they sneak a beer out of the fridge, and if their fathers notice, they convince their dads they must have already drank it themselves.

Some parents are more "cool," or at least try to be. They know that kids are going to drink—it's a rite of passage that they went through—and they believe it best if they do so at home. Though their motives might be good, this practice isn't without its own set of problems.

In many states, it is not illegal for a parent to serve alcohol to their own underage child; after all, law enforcement doesn't want to spend its time breaking up family dinners just because wine is served. But when parents provide alcohol to their child, it is often in the context of a party, and the alcohol is available to everyone present, including other minors. In most jurisdictions, this leaves the parents open to a criminal charge of contributing to the delinquency of a minor or endangering the welfare of a child. The other kids' parents could file civil charges against the host parents. If an accident should happen—or a fight break out—the host parents can be held partially responsible. Generally speaking, parents should probably be parents and not worry about being popular or "cool."

Stress and Advertising

Among teens, girls are beginning to outpace the boys as underage drinkers. Both boys and girls drink for the same reasons, but a 2004 study found that girls report more stress in their lives, leading them to drink alcohol. Included among the factors causing stress is the pressure to have sex. The same study found that some girls used alcohol to relieve their inhibitions about having sex.

A study conducted by Georgetown University in 2002 found that girls were more likely than boys to see ads for alcoholic beverages. These include ads equating sexy "bad" girls with alcohol.

Female teens are also being pitched new alcoholic products. Malt-based carbonated drinks (sometimes referred to as "alcopops") have innocent-sounding names—Skyy Blue, Breezer—and they look pretty. Though the company claims to be advertising to legal-age drinkers,

The teen years are a time of rebellion, when young adults are pushing limits and trying to express themselves. Sometimes this involves getting tattoos or piercings, and often drinking is a part of it as well.

the girls in the commercials look young enough that teenage girls might feel a kinship with them.

In the long run, it might not really matter why kids start drinking. It's the consequences that have a lasting effect.

Health Consequences

Teens are subject to the same alcohol-related health problems as adults. Results of a 2006 study, however, indicate that alcohol's effect on the brain might be more extensive in teens than originally believed. Studies on the brains of adolescent rats have shown that alcohol consumption produced significant cellular damage to their brains. Though it's too early to correlate those findings to humans, many researchers note similarities. Researchers have also found that alcoholic teens perform poorly on tests of verbal and nonverbal memory, attention focusing, and spatial skills.

Teenage girls are beginning to drink more often than teenage boys. One reason for this seems to be higher stress levels, in part the pressure to have sex.

As mentioned earlier in this book, the younger a person starts drinking alcohol, the higher the possibility of becoming an alcoholic as an adult. Unfortunately, many teens don't wait until they're adults; they become full-blown alcoholics while still in their teenage years, spending time in rehab rather than looking at colleges.

Binge drinking is popular among teens who choose to drink alcohol. Some teens are under the impression their behavior does not put them at risk of developing a problem with alcohol because they go through periods of not drinking. But, when they do binge, large quantities of alcohol are consumed in a relatively short period of time, sometimes leading to alcohol poisoning, a potentially fatal condition. When this happens, the body has become poisoned by such massive amounts of alcohol that it is unable to process it. Violent vomiting is the usually the first symptom. Other symptoms include extreme sleepiness, unconsciousness, difficulty breathing, dangerously low blood sugar, and *seizures*.

Alcohol and the Car

If drinking alcohol is considered a rite of passage, then getting a driver's license must seem like a constitutional right to some teens. Unfortunately, this combination of a rite and a right is a deadly one. According to the 2009 NSDUH Report, an estimated twelve percent of individuals aged twelve and older reported that they had driven under the influence of alcohol or illicit drugs at least once during the past year. Twenty-five percent of drivers between fifteen and twenty years of age who were killed in motor vehicle crashes in 2008 had a BAC of 0.08 or higher.

Coupled with the use of alcohol, driver inexperience is a major factor in these deaths. Most states have instituted

MADD

In 1980, Candy Lightner's life changed forever. Her thirteen-year-old daughter Cari was walking to a school carnival when a drunk driver hit her from behind, killing her. The driver had three drunk-driving convictions on his license and was out on bail for a hit-and-run arrest that had occurred just two days earlier.

Lightner did not let her life become consumed by grief over her daughter's death. Instead, she and a small group of friends decided to fight against drunk driving and work to get the states to pass stricter laws against it. Mothers Against Drunk Driving—MADD—has become one of the most successful grassroots efforts in history. The organization is credited with getting new laws and stiffer penalties in place throughout North America. One of their most successful efforts was to get the legal BAC level reduced to .08, which has saved countless lives. But perhaps most important, MADD changed the attitudes of a nation. Before Candy Lightner and MADD, drunk driving was often looked upon as a minor indiscretion, and at times, went unpunished. However, Candy Lightner put a face on what can happen as a result of drunk driving. It was the face of a thirteen-year-old, and drunk driving was no longer something that could be tossed off without consequence.

The influence of MADD didn't stop with adults. Initially founded as Students Against Driving Drunk in 1981, SADD is the dominant peer-to-peer youth education and prevention program operating in middle and high schools. In 1997, members of SADD requested that the national office change the group's mission to include other drugs, and the name was changed to Students Against Destructive Decisions. The organization advocates a "no use" policy for alcohol and drugs.

Each chapter designs its programs to meet the needs of their locales; what works in one community might not in another. Programs include workshops, leadership conferences, theme-focused forums, and awareness-raising activities. Groups also work to promote legislation that will aid in the achievement of their goals.

SADD's national organization has worked with state and federal agencies, nonprofit groups, and foundations to build leadership skills among teens, mobilize statewide collaboration among community partners, foster awareness of and support for youth initiatives, and organize efforts to promote youth health and safety. They have created a mighty and effective force.

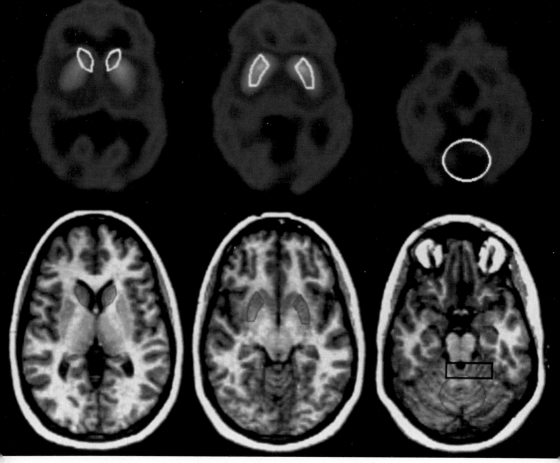

Alcohol has the same effects on teenage bodies as it does on adult bodies. However, recent studies have shown that alcohol may cause more extensive cellular damage to teenage brains.

some version of graduated driver licensing programs to help combat the inexperience factor. As young drivers gain experience, they are given more driving privileges, such as being able to drive at night and have friends as passengers.

Drinking as a teenager can lead down a dangerous and sad path. As is true for adults with alcoholism, for teens to get well, they must go through a treatment program.

7 Treatment of Alcohol Addiction

All addictions have at least one thing in common: the first step is to admit that you might need help. In some ways, this may be one of the hardest of a series of incredibly hard steps. But it is impossible to finish the journey to sobriety without taking that first step of admitting that you have a problem. Simply admitting to having a problem dealing with alcohol will get the treatment ball rolling, and the sooner treatment is begun, the greater its chance of success. And you don't have to be an alcoholic to seek treatment. Many people recognize they have a problem with alcohol and seek treatment, hoping to avoid falling into deeper problems.

One deterrent to getting help can be misconceptions about who alcoholics are. Sadly, the myth of the

There is no "type" of person who is an alcoholic; anyone is at risk. If you think you have a problem, don't be embarrassed to seek the help you need.

alcoholic as a weak person with low morals still exists in our society. The truth is that almost anyone who drinks can become an alcoholic. Talking to a health-care provider trained in treating alcohol-related problems can help someone overcome his sense of shame or embarrassment and allow treatment to begin.

The type of treatment will be determined in consultation with the health-care provider. It will be based on the severity of the problem and if the individual is already going through the withdrawal symptoms that come with detoxification. The most effective method of addiction treatment involves a multidisciplinary approach—and it doesn't happen over night.

Detoxification

When one decides to break free from addiction, the body must go through a process of withdrawal to rid itself of the toxic substances of the drug, in this case alcohol. Through a medically supervised process called detoxification, the individual goes through some or all of the withdrawal symptoms listed earlier in this book. If withdrawal symptoms are not too severe, the health-care provider may send the individual home with a four-day supply of an antianxiety medication such as a benzodiazepine. An appointment is made for follow-up and rehabilitation.

If withdrawal symptoms are more severe, such as when the individual has DTs, seizures, or *hallucinations*, hospitalization is generally required so that medication can be given and the individual monitored.

When it's time to choose a treatment philosophy, there are two primary methods of treating addiction: behavioral and *pharmacological*.

Behavioral Treatment Programs

Put simply, behavioral treatment programs teach people with addictions to change their behaviors so they are less likely to repeat those that led to addiction in the first place. Unfortunately, nothing about addiction is simple. Though behavioral treatment programs do help those with addictions find ways to avoid behaviors that can

After the body has gone through detoxification, the individual must then choose a treatment method to deal with the addiction. Cognitive-behavioral therapy attempts to change behavior patterns by discovering how thoughts influence behaviors.

cause a relapse, they also need to help these individuals discover what led to those behaviors initially. **Cognitive-behavioral therapy** helps the individuals recognize how thought patterns influence behaviors. With therapy, individuals learn how to change negative thought patterns, and thereby how to change behaviors. Individual and family therapy can help the person with addiction and those around her learn how to cope with life as a recovering alcoholic. Therapy can also help the individual and her family and friends handle relapses; most people do relapse at some point during recovery.

Behavioral treatment programs also help those with addictions handle life without alcohol. After all, alcohol and drinking are all around. Though some programs work under the premise that recovering alcoholics can drink in moderation without threatening their sobriety, North American doctors question its *efficacy*. Most doctors and alcohol counselors in North America are convinced that the best treatment results are achieved when the individual practices abstinence from alcohol.

For some individuals, behavioral treatment programs work better if the person is an inpatient. Depending on the length and severity of addiction, inpatient treatment can be short-term (usually a minimum of thirty days) or long-term residential. At first, some programs allow inpatients to have minimal—if any—contact with the "outside world." Patients concentrate on learning about themselves and their relationship with alcohol. Later, family and perhaps close friends are encouraged to participate in the treatment program.

Pharmacological Treatment Programs

Medications can be effective in treating alcohol addiction. *Opioid antagonists* reduce the intoxicating effects—the buzz—of alcohol. The most commonly used ones in the treatment of alcoholism are naltrexone and nalmefene. Both help prevent relapse, naltrexone in low- to moderate drinkers and nalmefene for heavier drinkers. The drugs work only if the individual is still drinking; once a patient stops, the drugs are no longer effective. Both are

Brand Name vs. Generic Name

Talking about medications can be confusing because every drug has at least two names: its "generic name" and the "brand name" that the pharmaceutical company uses to market the drug. Generic names are based on the drug's chemical structure, while drug companies use brand names to inspire public recognition and loyalty for their products.

more beneficial if the individual is also receiving psychological counseling, such as cognitive-behavioral therapy.

Another type of drug used to treat alcohol abuse is disulfiram, sold under the brand name Antabuse®. Disulfiram is an **aversion drug**; it interacts with alcohol to produce very unpleasant side effects, such as nausea, vomiting, and headaches. Just a half a glass of wine combined with Antabuse can produce the symptoms, which last from one to two hours, depending on the dose of disulfiram and the amount of alcohol consumed. Studies have shown that the drug is most effective if the individual has someone around who will make sure that he takes it.

Antidepressants such as Prozac® or Zoloft® may be prescribed to treat depression. Depression is very common in people with alcoholism and alcohol abuse problems, and depression can contribute to relapse. Some evidence indicates that these antidepressants may reduce cravings for alcohol, but the primary indicator for their prescription is the presence of depression.

Most treatment programs use a combination of behavioral treatment and pharmacological methods. Individuals are also encouraged to supplement their programs with support groups such as Alcoholics Anonymous.

Alcoholics Anonymous

Alcoholics Anonymous (AA) was founded in 1935, and has grown to become the best-known and most successful program for helping people who have problems with alcohol. Today, there are chapters all over the world. AA's books and pamphlets are published in more than thirty languages.

Each chapter's program is based on the original twelve steps that have become synonymous with AA. These steps have a spiritual component, and some people object to this, but many studies have proven the value of some form of prayer and meditation to a recovery program. AA emphasizes that the Higher Power referred to in the steps

Alcoholics Anonymous, or AA, has become well known as a successful program for helping people overcome problems with alcohol. An important part of the program is attendance at and participation in AA meetings.

does not refer to any particular belief system; it can mean what the individual wants—and needs—it to mean.

The twelve steps are:

1. We admitted we were powerless over alcohol—that our lives had become unmanageable.
2. Came to believe that a Power greater than ourselves could restore us to sanity.
3. Made a decision to turn our will and our lives over to the care of God as we understand Him.
4. Made a searching and fearless moral inventory of ourselves.
5. Admitted to God, and to ourselves, and to another human being the exact nature of our wrongs.
6. We're entirely ready to have God remove all these defects of character.
7. Humbly asked Him to remove our shortcomings.
8. Made a list of all persons we had harmed, and became willing to make amends to them all.
9. Made direct amends to such people wherever possible, except when to do so would injure them or others.
10. Continued to take personal inventory and when we were wrong promptly admitted it.
11. Sought through prayer and meditation to improve our conscious contact with God as we understand Him, praying only for knowledge of His will for us and the power to carry that out.
12. Having had a spiritual awakening as the result of these steps, we tried to carry this message to other alcoholics and to practice these principles in all our affairs.

Though attendance at and participation in AA meetings will not guarantee a recovery free from temptation

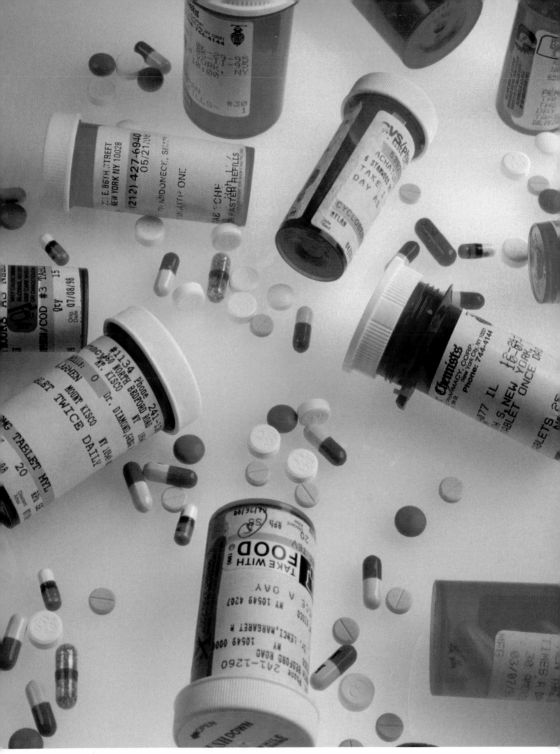

Pharmacological treatment of alcoholism involves taking medication to reduce the "buzz" caused by alcohol, or to produce unpleasant side effects if the patient has a drink. These drugs work best when the patient is undergoing behavioral treatment as well.

What Do Rehab Programs Accomplish?

Abstinence

In many cases it seems that as long as the substance is in the blood stream, thinking remains distorted. Often during the first days or weeks of total abstinence, we see a gradual clearing of thinking processes. This is a complex psychological and biological phenomenon, and is one of the elements that inpatient programs are able to provide by making sure the patient is fully detoxified and remains abstinent during his or her stay.

Removal of Denial

In some cases, when someone other than the patient, such as a parent, employer, or other authority, is convinced there is a problem, but the addict is not yet sure, voluntary attendance at a rehab program will provide enough clarification to remove this basic denial. Even those who are convinced they have a problem with substances usually don't admit to themselves or others the full extent of the addiction. Rehab uses group process to identify and help the individual to let go of these expectable forms of denial.

Removal of Isolation

As addictions progress, relationships deteriorate in quality. However, the bonds between fellow recovering people are widely recognized as one of the few forces powerful enough to keep recovery on track. The rehab experience, whether it is inpatient or outpatient involves in-depth sharing in a group setting. This kind of sharing creates strong interpersonal bonds among group members. These bonds help to form a support system that will be powerful enough to sustain the individual during the first months of abstinence.

"Basic Training"

Basic training is a good way to think of the experience of rehab. Soldiers need a rapid course to give them the basic knowledge and skills they will need to fight in a war. Some kinds of learning need to be practiced so well that you can do them without thinking. In addition to the learning, trainees become physically fit, and perhaps most important, form emotional bonds that help keep up morale when the going is hard.

(*Source*: Partnership for a Drug-Free America)

As with any major life change, a recovering alcoholic will need the support of family and friends as she readjusts to a life without alcohol. Family and friends may also want to seek guidance and support at groups such as Al-Anon and Alateen.

and relapse, AA meetings can play an important role in staying sober.

AA recognizes the importance of family and friends to the person as she adjusts to life as a recovering alcoholic. Al-Anon and Alateen operate as support groups for friends and families, helping those involved with the recovering alcoholic deal with the changes as well as realize they are not alone on their journey.

Having an addiction to alcohol does not make one less of a person. It does create a person with a problem. But,

Is Alcohol Always Bad?

No, it isn't. Research has found that one to two drinks per day IN ADULTS can provide health benefits and longer life (unless there is a reason not to drink such as alcoholism, liver disease, other drugs, etc.). However, alcohol is never beneficial to children and young adults.

most people do have problems of one sort or another. It's part of what makes us human. Knowing when and how to deal with whatever problems one has is the key to a successful life. The road is long and hard, but we can all find ways to overcome the problems we encounter.

Glossary

abstinence: Habitually refraining from something, in this case drinking alcoholic beverages.

angst: A feeling of anxiety, apprehension, or insecurity.

attachment: An emotional bond or tie to somebody.

attention deficit disorder: A condition occurring mainly in children, characterized by hyperactivity, inability to concentrate, and impulsive behavior.

auxiliaries: Groups organized to support or supplement another group.

aversion drug: A chemical prescribed because it causes unpleasant sensations in the patient when combined with alcohol.

bacchanals: Noisy, drunken celebrations.

blood-brain barrier: A membrane that controls the passage of substances from the blood into the brain. It is permeable to alcohol.

cognitive-behavioral therapy: A treatment method that encourages patients to confront and challenge their distorted thinking methods, thereby changing behavior.

compulsory: Required.

decadent: Showing uninhibited, self-indulgent behavior.

efficacy: The ability to produce the necessary or desired results.

electrons: Subatomic particles carrying a negative charge.

endocrine: Relating to the glands that secrete hormones internally, directly into the lymph or bloodstream.

episodic: Divided into connected but independent sections.

excite: Raise something above its lowest energy level to a higher one.

extremist: Someone who holds extreme or radical political or religious beliefs.

formaldehyde: A colorless gas that is used in making resins and fertilizers.

futility: An action that has no use, purpose, or effect.

genetic: Involving characteristics that can be passed by heredity.

germinate: To be created and start to develop, as in seeds sprouting.

hallucinations: Perceptions of somebody or something that is not really there.

heretics: Those who hold an opinion that contradicts established religious teaching.

hypothesize: To give a tentative explanation for a phenomenon.

impotence: The inability of a male to perform sexual intercourse.

inebriation: The condition of being drunk or intoxicated.

inhibit: To stop something from happening.

lobbying: To attempt to persuade a political representative or influential person to support or fight a particular cause.

Macedonians: People who were citizens of the ancient kingdom of Macedonia.

mass: The religious ceremony of the Communion.

mead: An alcoholic drink made by fermenting honey with water, often with added spices.

metabolism: The ongoing interrelated series of chemical interactions taking place in living organisms that provide the energy and nutrients needed to sustain life.

moderation: The state of not becoming extreme or excessive.

neurodevelopment: The growth of the nervous system.

neurosensory: Relating to the sensory activity of nerve cells or the nervous system.

opioid antagonists: Chemicals that diminish the effects of opium-containing substances produced in the brain.

pancreatitis: Inflamation of the pancreas.

pharmacological: Relating to the study of drugs.

Pharmacopoeia: A book or database listing drugs used in medical practice and describing their composition, preparation, use, dosages, effect, and side effects.

pictographs: Graphic symbols representing a word or idea.

polytheistic: The belief in more than one god.

postoperative: Occurring after surgery.

Prohibition: The U.S. government ban on alcoholic beverages.

ratification: Official approval.

repealed: Officially revoked something such as a law.

replete: Having enough to be fully satisfied.

seizures: Abnormal electrical discharges in the brain.

Shabbat: The Jewish Sabbath, the day of rest and reflection beginning at sundown on Friday and lasting until sundown on Saturday.

sommelier: A waiter in a restaurant who has charge of wines and their service.

speakeasies: Clubs where alcoholic beverages were sold and consumed illegally during Prohibition.

staff of life: Food, generally considered to be bread, that is considered to be an essential part of the human diet.

Stone Age: The earliest period of human history.

temperance: Total abstinence from alcoholic drink.

vetoed: One branch of government officially rejecting the legislation of another.

viticulture: The science or practice of growing grapevines, particularly for making wine.

Further Reading

Alagna, Magdalena, and Ruth Anne Ruiz. *Everything You Need to Know About the Dangers of Binge Drinking*. New York: Rosen, 2001.

Armstrong, Elizabeth, and Christina McCarroll. "The New Face of Underage Drinking: Teenage Girls." *Christian Science Monitor*, July 8, 2004.

Barbour, Scott. *Alcohol*. Farmington Hills, Mich.: Thomson Gale, 2005.

Clayton, Lawrence. *Alcohol Drug Dangers*. Berkeley Heights, N.J.: Enslow, 2001.

Danner, Patrick. "Broward County: Alcohol Industry Accused of Marketing to Minors." *Miami Herald*, April 14, 2005.

Egendorf, Laura K., Bonnie Szumski, Scott Barbour, and Brenda Stalcup, eds. *Teen Alcoholism*. Farmington Hills, Mich.: Thomson Gale, 2001.

Esherick, Joan. *Dying for Acceptance: A Teen's Guide to Drug- and Alcohol-Related Health Issues*. Broomall, Pa.: Mason Crest, 2004.

Harvey, Haisong. *Alcohol Abuse*. Farmington Hills, Mich.: Thomson Gale, 2002.

"Helplessness to Hope: My War with Chemical, and Other, Weapons of Destruction." *UN Chronicle*, June 22, 1998.

House, Dawn. "Program Targets Teenage Drinkers with Prevention Message." *Salt Lake Tribune*, December 17, 2005.

Konieczko, Craig. *Intervention: Putting Yourself Between a Friend and Addiction*. New York: Rosen, 2000.

Lamb, Kirsten, and Wendy Lamb. *Alcohol*. Milwaukee, Wis.: Raintree Publishers, 2002.

Libal, Joyce. *Drug Therapy and Substance-Related Disorders*. Broomall, Pa.: Mason Crest, 2004.

Marshall, Shelly. Young, *Sober and Free: Teen-to-Teen Stories of Hope and Recovery*. Center City, Minn.: Hazelden, 2003.

Richards, Pam G., and Sean Connolly. *Alcohol*. Portsmouth, N.H.: Heinemann, 2000.

Rosengren, John, and Alcoholics Anonymous. *Big Book Unplugged: A Young Person's Guide to Alcoholics Anonymous*. Center City, Minn.: Hazelden, 2003.

Seely, Hart. "When Teenagers Die, Communities Begin to Question Alcoholic Rites of Passage." *Post-Standard* (Syracuse, N.Y.), March 8, 2005.

Snyder, Gail. *Teens & Alcohol*. Broomall, Pa.: Mason Crest, 2004.

"Taking a Hard Line Against Teenage Drinking." *Washington Post*, May 20, 2004.

"Teenage Girls Targeted for Sweet-Flavored Alcoholic Beverages: Polls Show More Teen Girls See 'Alcopop' Ads Than Women Age 21–44." *U.S. Newswire*, December 16, 2004.

Tomson, Ellen. "Alcopops—Cute, Boozy and Pitched to Teenage Girls." *Saint Paul Pioneer Press*, April 21, 2006.

Torr, James D. *Alcoholism*. Farmington Hills, Mich.: Gale Group, 2000.

Volkmann, Chris, and Toren Volkmann. *From Binge to Blackout: A Mother and Son Struggle With Teen Drinking*. New York: Penguin, 2006.

For More Information

Al-Anon/Alateen
www.al-anon.alateen.org

Alcohol: Teens Health Answers & Advice
kidshealth.com/teen/drug_alcohol/alcohol/alcohol.html

Alcoholics Anonymous
www.aa.org

Drinking: Facts for Teens
familydoctor.org/online/famdocen/home/common/addictions/alcohol/273.html

SADD (Students Against Destructive Decisions, formerly Students Against Driving Drunk)
www.sadd.org

The Cool Spot: The Young Teen's Place for Info on Alcohol and Resisting Peer Pressure
www.thecoolspot.gov

The websites listed on this page were active at the time of publication. The publisher is not responsible for websites that have changed their addresses or discontinued operation since the date of publication. The publisher will review and update the website list upon each reprint.

Bibliography

"Alcohol and Teen Drinking." Focus Adolescent Services. http://www.focusas.com/Alcohol.html.

"Alcohol on Campus." Teen Drug Abuse. http://teendrugabuse.us/teenalcoholabuse.html.

Alcohol: Problems and Solutions. http://www2.Potsdam.edu/hansondj/FunFacts/index.html.

"Alcoholism." Cleveland Clinic Health Information Center. http://www.clevelandclinic.org/health/health-info/docs/0000/0011.asp.

"Alcoholism." http://www.reutershealth.com/wellconnected/doc56.html.

Armstrong, Elizabeth, and Christina McCarroll. "The New Face of Underage Drinking: Teenage Girls." *Christian Science Monitor*, July 8, 2004.

Arnst, Catherine. "Can Alcoholism be Treated?" *Business Week*, April 11, 2005.

Butler, Katy. "The Grim Neurology of Teenage Drinking." *New York Times*, July 4, 2006.

Canadian Health Network. "How Does Alcohol Affect Health?" http://www.Canadian-health-network.ca.

"History of Alcohol and Drinking Around the World." Alcohol: Problems and Solutions. http://www2.Potsdam.edu.hansondj/Controversies/1114796842.html.

"I Was a Teen Alcoholic." *Seventeen*, March 1974.

Loyola Marymount University. "History of Alcohol Use." HeadsUP! http://www.lmu.edu/headsup/students/history.html.

Marus, Robert. "Baptist History on Alcohol: Not Totally Teetotaling." http://www.abpnews.com/1107.article.

Mentalhealth Channel. "Alcohol Abuse & Dependence." http://www.mentalhealthchannel.net.

Milton S. Hershey Medical Center, College of Medicine, Penn State University. "Alcoholism and Alcohol Abuse." http://www.hmc.psu.edu/healthinfo/a/alsoholism.htm.

National Institute on Alcohol Abuse and Alcoholism. *Alcoholism: Getting the Facts*. Washington, D.C.: U.S. Department of Health and Human Services, National Institutes of Health, 2004.

National Organization on Fetal Alcohol Syndrome. "Identifying Individuals With Prenatal Alcohol Exposure." http://www.nofas.org/healthcare/identify.aspx.

National Organization on Fetal Alcohol Syndrome. "Screening Patients for Alcohol Use." http://www.nofas.org/healthcare/screen.aspx.

National Organization on Fetal Alcohol Syndrome. "Treating Individuals Affected With FASD." http://www.nofas.org/healthcare/treatment.aspx.

Partnership for a Drug-Free America. "Why Teenagers Use—and Abuse—Alcohol and Other Drugs." http://www.drugfree.org.

Student Wellness Program. http://umr.edu/wellness/alcoholism.html.

Substance Abuse and Mental Health Services Administration. Results from the 2004 National Survey on Drug Use and Health: National Findings (Office of Applied Studies, NSDUH Series H-28. DHHS Publication No. SMA 054062). Rockville, Md.: Author.

"Teen Drinking Takes Toll on Brian: Study Shows Effects of Alcohol Can Last Far Longer Than Expected." CBS Evening News, July 5, 2006. http://www.cbsnews.com/stories/2006/07/05/eveningnews.main177.html.

Teen Drug Abuse. "The Health Effects of Teen Alcohol Use." http://www.teendrugabuse.us/teensandalcohol.html.

"Teenage Drinking Tied to Lifelong Alcohol Woes." MSNBC.com. http://www.msnbc.msn.com/is/13737847.

Thompson, Jessica. "Teens Gather in D.C. to Say: Keep Us Free of Drugs, Alcohol; Minnesota Youth Had Personal Stories to Tell as the Group SADD Launched a New Anti-Drinking Campaign." *Star Tribune* (Minneapolis, Minn.), July 18, 2001.

University of Oklahoma Police Department. *The Police Notebook.* Norman: University of Oklahoma, 2005.

Index

Picture Credits

Artville
    Boyajian, Ann: p. 80
    Smallish, Craig: p. 106
Bananastock: p. 93
Clipart.com: p. 109
Comstock: p. 49
Corel Professional Photos: p. 21, 25
Corbis: p. 84
ImageSource: p. 104, 111
istock.com
    Byron, Robert: p. 90
    kkgas: p. 50
    Monu, Nicholas: p. 64
    Spauln: p. 63
Miller, Malinda: pp. 10, 60
PhotoDisc: pp. 8, 71, 78, 83, 101
Photolink
    Pearce, S: p. 86
Photos.com: pp. 12, 18, 23, 38, 54, 57, 67, 68, 72, 75, 77, 102, 113
Stockbyte: pp. 58, 88, 97, 98
Thinkstock: p. 94

Author and Consultant Biographies

Author

Ida Walker is a graduate of the University of Northern Iowa in Cedar Falls, and has done graduate work at Syracuse University. The author of several nonfiction books, she currently lives in Upstate New York.

Series Consultant

Jack E. Henningfield, Ph.D., is a professor at the Johns Hopkins University School of Medicine, and he is also Vice President for Research and Health Policy at Pinney Associates, a consulting firm in Bethesda, Maryland, that specializes in science policy and regulatory issues concerning public health, medications development, and behavior-focused disease management. Dr. Henningfield has contributed information relating to addiction to numerous reports of the U.S. Surgeon General, the National Academy of Sciences, and the World Health Organization.